My Emotions Through Emojis

FEELING EXCITED

BY
THEIA LAKE

Enslow
PUBLISHING

Please visit our website, www.enslow.com.
For a free color catalog of all our high-quality books, call toll free 1-800-398-2504 or fax 1-877-980-4454.

Cataloging-in-Publication Data
Names: Lake, Theia.
Title: Feeling excited / Theia Lake.
Description: New York : Enslow Publishing, 2024. | Series: My emotions through emojis | Includes index.
Identifiers: ISBN 9781978533363 (pbk.) | ISBN 9781978533370 (library bound) | ISBN 9781978533387 (ebook)
Subjects: LCSH: Elation–Juvenile literature. | Agitation (Psychology)–Juvenile literature. | Emotions in children–Juvenile literature.
Classification: LCC BF575.E5 L35 2023 | DDC 155.4'1242–dc23

Published in 2024 by
Enslow Publishing
2544 Clinton Street
Buffalo, NY 14224

Designer: Tanya Dellaccio Keeney
Editor: Theresa Emminizer

Photo credits: Cover (phone) Victor Z/Shutterstock.com; cover, series art (clouds) Theus/Shutterstock.com; cover, series art (emojis) stas11/Shutterstock.com; p. 5 Khosro/Shutterstock.com; p. 7 Prostock-studio/Shutterstock.com; p. 9 Roman Samborskyi/Shutterstock.com; p. 11 Africa Studio/Shutterstock.com; p. 13 Krakenimages.com/Shutterstock.com; p. 15 stockfour/Shutterstock.com; p. 17 EZ-Stock Studio/Shutterstock.com; p. 19 BearFotos/Shutterstock.com; p. 21 Monkey Business Images/Shutterstock.com.

Printed in the United States of America

CPSIA compliance information: Batch #CS24ENS: For further information contact Enslow Publishing, at 1-800-398-2504.

CONTENTS

Get Excited! 4
Getting What You Want 6
How Does It Feel? 8
Doing What You Love 10
What Excites You? 12
Too Much Excitement! 14
Be Considerate 16
Taking Turns 18
A Great Feeling 20
Words to Know 22
For More Information 23
Index 24

Boldface words appear in Words to Know.

GET EXCITED!

When you're excited, you might have butterflies in your stomach. You feel happy. You feel hopeful. You feel bright!

We're often excited when we're looking forward to something fun, such as a birthday! What do you get excited about?

GETTING WHAT YOU WANT

Erin has always wanted to go to summer camp. This year, for the first time ever, she finally gets to go 😁!

Erin calls her friends. They're excited too 🤗! They talk about all the fun things they'll do together at camp.

HOW DOES IT FEEL?

When you're excited, you might feel like you can't keep still! Your heart is beating very fast. Your body is filled with **energy**!

Maybe you jump up and down! Maybe you clap your hands. Maybe you do a little dance!

DOING WHAT YOU LOVE

Felix loved to **perform**. His school was having a **talent show**, and he was putting on an act.

Felix felt a little nervous 😣. But he was excited too 😃! When Felix was on **stage**, he felt like he was at his very best 😊!

WHAT EXCITES YOU?

Is there something that you love doing? Something that makes you feel happy and lively? Something that makes you feel like you're at your best?

Every person is **unique**. We all have different things that make us feel excited. What's something that excites you?

TOO MUCH EXCITEMENT!

Rory was showing his friend Matt his favorite movie of all time. Rory was so excited 😁! As they watched, he talked and talked.

Soon, Matt got mad 😡. It was his first time seeing this movie. He didn't want Rory to talk through the whole thing!

BE CONSIDERATE

When you're really excited about something, it can be easy to lose control. You might talk a lot. Your voice might get loud.

It's important to be **considerate** of how others feel. Give others time and space to share what they're excited about too!

TAKING TURNS

Nova and Teddy love playing together 😊😊. They're both good at taking turns. They're both good sports.

When Nova wins, she's excited! She cheers 🤗! Then she shakes Teddy's hand. It's exciting to win. But having fun together is the best part of all!

A GREAT FEELING

Feeling excited is great! It makes us feel **alive**. It makes us feel happy. It makes us want to make things and do things!

When you're excited, enjoy it! But make sure to be considerate of others' feelings too.

WORDS TO KNOW

alive: Full of life.

considerate: Thoughtful about others' feelings.

energy: Liveliness.

perform: To carry out an action.

stage: A place where people perform a show.

talent show: A show or competition showing off a skill or gift.

unique: One of a kind.

FOR MORE INFORMATION

BOOKS

Bromage, Fran. *I Can Feel*. New York, NY: Windmill Books, 2023.

Wood, John. *Harry the Hamster Feels Happy*. New York, NY: Windmill Books, 2020.

WEBSITES

Kids Health
kidshealth.org/en/kids/talk-feelings.html
Learn how to name and talk about your feelings.

PBS Kids
pbskids.org/arthur/health/resilience/draw-your-feelings.html
Try out fun activities to express your emotions!

Publisher's note to educators and parents: Our editors have carefully reviewed these websites to ensure that they are suitable for students. Many websites change frequently, however, and we cannot guarantee that a site's future contents will continue to meet our high standards of quality and educational value. Be advised that students should be closely supervised whenever they access the internet.

INDEX

consideration, 16, 20
energy, 8
fun, 6, 18
happy, 4, 12, 20
hopeful, 4
loud, 16
mad, 14
nervous, 10